Mary Madalene

a Woman of Resilience

5 Lessons to Develop an
Irrepressible Passion for Jesus

The Irrepressible Disciple Series
Book 1

Mary Rodman

Published by:
Legacy Lane Publishing
Weatherford, TX
www.LegacyLanePublishing.com
ISBN: 978-1-7331234-4-0

How to use this Bible study

I encourage you to spend time in prayer before and after each lesson. Ask God to open your mind and soul to the message before you start. Seek His blessings as you apply the lesson to your life afterward.

Please take notes as you read and contemplate the questions. I am a firm believer that journaling is a wonderful concept, so grab a journal and record your thoughts! It leaves a path of your Christian journey, which you can read over and over.

Your Bible study can be used one of two ways.

1. **Individually** - Read one lesson each morning or allow more time between the lessons to apply God's truths to your life.

2. **Group** - One or two lessons each week are recommended. Conversations and discussions with others will always provide more insight on the lessons. You will be amazed how each message speaks differently to others.

Please follow me on Social Media as MrsMaryRodman and leave a post at www.facebook.com/MrsMaryRodman. I love to meet new people and will answer any questions you may have.

Enjoy your Bible study!

Mary

Table of Contents

Lesson 1: A Wealthy Woman

I often wonder what it would be like to speak directly with some of the great saints of the Bible. I want to ask Peter how it felt to walk on water. For Paul I wonder, what was the thorn in his flesh? Was it a physical ailment, mental struggle, or a spiritual battle? But of all the New Testament servants of Christ, Mary Magdalene is one who seems the most mysterious to me.

Not mysterious as in secretive. Mysterious because I want to know—where did she find the strength to do all she accomplished for Jesus? We are first introduced to Mary in the *Luke 8*.

Read *Luke 8:1-3*

We have no other background about Mary Magdalene, except that Jesus performed a great miracle in her life. What else is there to say? Christ dramatically changed her life when He cast the demons from her. Once Mary discovered her Savior, she was totally committed to Him with a servant's heart. She became one of Jesus' followers and part of His road crew, so to speak. She worked behind the scenes and provided financial support for His ministry. Gratitude obviously flowed from her soul as she expressed her love for Jesus.

The scriptures say the ladies who traveled with Jesus and his disciples helped support them financially. This indicates Mary was from a wealthy family. She was so in love with Jesus, that she gave to Christ's ministry without question.

1. Which do you feel is more important and why? Your financial support to God's church, missions, and ministry—or your compassion, love and concern for others?

Read *Matthew 23:23-24*

In this passage of scripture, Jesus states that tithing is important, but He puts a greater emphasis on how the Pharisees treated others. Jesus points his finger at their hypocrisy. He is also speaking to us in this scripture. We cannot give financially and neglect doing God's work. Caring for others within the congregation, the community, and the world is what we are commissioned to do.

There are times in our lives when both tithing and compassion can be difficult for Christians. You may be financially strapped and wish you could support the ministry of the church more. Sometimes your mental state is overloaded due to the stress of life. Many also suffer from Christian burnout due to over commitment.

2. In those seasons of life when you feel you have nothing left to give, how do you recover? (Examples: Pray, a hobby, rest, focus on nature, you fill in the blank.)

Read *Psalm 46:10*

3. How does God tell you to recover?

Read *Matthew 11:28-30*

4. Where should you find the strength to serve again?

When you are in a season of financial difficulties, you often feel guilty because you are not able to support the church and missions as your heart desires.

Read *Luke 21:1-4*

5. What does this scripture tell you about tithing?

God calls you to tithe, but only if your tithe is with a gracious heart. It isn't about your financial status or your ability to give large amounts of money. When it comes to serving Christ, and that includes tithing, everything you do is about the heart. There is a huge difference between giving financially and giving financially out of love. Financial giving and serving others—are both about the heart.

Yes, Mary Magdalene, was a wealthy woman, but she also possessed a servant's heart. In the next lesson, we will dig deeper into Mary Magdalene's servant heart and begin to understand exactly how she was able to serve others endlessly.

Your Challenge

When you tithe, what is the condition of your heart? Spend time in prayer and ask the Lord to reveal the condition of your heart when you give—financially, emotionally, and physically to God's ministry.

Journal your thoughts on this lesson.

Give It Your All

At a recent event known as the Walk to Emmaus I was blessed to be on the leadership team and help lead discussions with some wonderful ladies. On our last day, we asked one another about our favorite Bible story. For me it was so hard to choose. You have the story of Esther. The Samaritan Woman. The woman who touched Jesus' robe. Peter walked on water. How do you choose just one? I admit I don't remember which one I selected, but I remember Iola's favorite. It was the widow woman's offering.

This short story in the Bible wasn't even on my top ten list, so when Iola mentioned this story it piqued my interest. I have always felt that Jim and I are good financial stewards, so these few verses never made much of an impact. I always read them with pride in my heart. Give financially, yep done, checked off my list of good deeds. What an attitude, because the story is about much more than financial stewardship!

> *While Jesus was in the Temple, he watched the rich people dropping their gifts in the collection box. Then a poor widow came by and dropped in two small coins. "I tell you the truth," Jesus said, "this poor widow has given more than all the rest of them. For they have given a tiny part of their surplus, but she, poor as she is, has given everything she has." Luke 21:1-4*

I read these verses several times over the next couple of days, and studied the footnotes in my Bible. God calls for us to give our all. Not just financially, but in every area of our lives. I am now convicted every time I read, *"For they have given a tiny part of their surplus, but she, poor as she is, has given everything she has."* Jesus calls us to give all of our time to serve others. All of our strength for the trials in life. All of our compassion for the hurting. All of our gifts and talents. In every area of our lives, we should take intentional steps to give all we have to Christ.

In these verses, Jesus isn't concerned about a money issue. He is concerned about a heart issue. The widow wasn't blessed because she gave financially. She was blessed because she gave from her heart. She reminds me of David, a man after God's own heart. (*1 Samuel 13:14*). She was a woman after God's own heart. She wasn't a woman who simply gave monetarily. She was a woman who invested in the kingdom of God with all of her heart, all of her mind, and all of her soul. *(Matthew 22:37).*

> Dear Lord,
> I ask your forgiveness for my foolish pride and for the time I spend on worldly items, which do not point others to Christ. Change my heart Lord, so I desire to serve You with my whole heart, my whole mind, and my whole soul. Help me to use my gifts and my talents within your church, and the ministries which bless You. Lord give me strength to go above and beyond what I feel is possible each day, because with You everything is possible.

Please help me grow stronger in my faith and become a Christian who desires to see others as You see them. Make me more like the Widow Woman and turn me into a woman who is after God's own heart. You have asked for my best Lord, and for today, I give You my all.

In Jesus' name, Amen.

Excerpt from *Live Life in Full Bloom*

Mary's greatest joy is helping others cultivate and grow their relationship with Christ. Part of her ministry is her devotional books: *Bloom Where You're Planted* and *Live Life in Full Bloom* and *Bloom in God's Promises*. Purchase your *Bloom Daily Devotional Series* with matching journals at www.MaryRodman.com/Shop

Mary Rodman

Lesson 2: A Servant of Christ

Mary Magdalene and the other ladies were behind the scenes people. In modern day terms, you could call them Jesus' road crew. They were His silent ministry support staff and they helped in every way possible. These ladies most likely had the spiritual gift of helps. As we study further, you will see that Mary possessed many spiritual gifts, but this lesson is on servanthood.

It was common in those days for women to be treated as second class citizens, but Christ never treated women in that manner, and Mary Magdalene was no exception. Jesus saw how resilient Mary was and her deep commitment to His ministry. So, from the moment He healed her of her demons, He treated Mary Magdalene as chosen, precious, beloved, royalty.

As a result of all Christ did for her, Mary chose to be part of Christ's support staff. She was a little bit like Martha, except she joyfully did the behind the scenes work without the whining and complaining. Her servant's heart had no room for petty problems or disagreements. She graciously served her Savior.

Reread *Luke 8:1-3*

1. Why do you think Mary willingly served behind the scenes as part of Jesus' road crew.

Read *2 Timothy 2:24*

2. How does this verse describe a servant?

When the scriptures say **teach** many of us turn and run from servanthood! Not everyone feels qualified to teach the scriptures, myself included. I have no divinity degree and I'm not a person who can quote scripture after scripture providing an answer for your situation. However, I am able to use the Concordance and www.biblegateway.com to research the Bible for answers.

What I teach are life lessons. Through my devotions, I share how Jesus impacts my life, over and over again. I pray my words in this study will help you grow as a servant of Christ. When you and I grow as a Christian on our own, we are able to teach others. Therefore, we are **all** called to teach.

Teaching simply means, find your niche and excel at it! Teach children. Teach patience. Show compassion. Cook a meal. Visit a shut-in. Your actions as a servant are teachable moments. In other words, don't be a servant alone. Bring someone beside you and teach them how to serve with a willing heart.

Mary Magdalene became a servant because she walked with Jesus and learned from Him. Maybe it was easier for her to show compassion because she witnessed Christ's empathy on a daily basis. Or maybe it was more difficult because she walked with the Servant himself.

Did she have moments of doubt when she compared herself to Christ? Was her servant's heart strong enough to carry the load? How and why did she continually serve behind the scenes?

To understand Mary Magdalene's resilient servant's heart, read each verse carefully and note the key meaning of each one.

3. How can each biblical principle make you a more resilient person? Journal your thoughts.

Psalm 18:1
> God is my strength

Lamentations 3:32
> God is compassionate and loving

Psalm 84:11
> The Lord gives us grace and mercy

Habakkuk 3:18
> The Lord is our salvation

Micah 6:8
> Walk humbly with the Lord

Proverbs 3:5-6
> Trust the Lord

Mark 10:45
> Christ came to serve

Mary Magdalene knew and understood:

- Christ was also a servant. We serve others, because Christ first served us.
- Trust the Lord in all circumstances. Trust and faith go hand in hand as we build a stronger relationship with Christ.
- God gives strength to the weary when we carry a heavy load. He doesn't expect us to serve alone. We need to work together and He is with us to help carry the load.
- He offers grace when we stumble. We aren't perfect! We are going to make mistakes, but grace will cover us when we fall.
- His compassion and love are unending. Mary Magdalene witnessed this unending compassion and tapped into the strength it gave her.
- We are called to walk and serve with a humble heart. A humble heart brings us back to Lesson 1. Serve because you want to, not because you have to.
- Jesus is our salvation when we believe and trust in Him.

Mary Magdalene was a witness to these truths each and every day as she journeyed with Christ. Her Biblical knowledge gave her strength to accomplish ministry. She didn't serve behind the scenes because she had to, Mary served as a gift to Christ. Her love for her Savior was the driving force in her life and it overflowed into her ministry. She not only gave financially, she gave financially and served with a servant's heart.

As I asked before, why did Mary Magdalene willingly serve behind the scenes as part of Jesus' road crew? She served out of love, because Jesus set her free! We will look into Mary's freedom in Lesson 3 and learn more about this freedom which Christ offers us.

Your Challenge

Pinpoint areas of service where your gifts and talents will best serve Christ. Make notes about ways to enhance your ministry, teach others, and serve with a servant's heart.

Journal your thoughts on this lesson.

Leah's Dedication

My mother-in-law, Leah, took great pride in attending all of her grandchildren's events. They spent their winters in Florida, but if she was in Ohio, she never missed a ballgame, a pig show, a band concert, or a choir performance. Even though she occasionally paid the price for her attendance, her dedication to her grandchildren was endless.

Jim often laughs about the time she was in a horrible mood for several days. He finally confronted her about her attitude, and she confessed she had received a speeding ticket on the way to her granddaughter's choir performance. She was clocked driving seventy miles per hour in a thirty-five mile per hour zone! She had never had a speeding ticket before and began to cry because her name would be printed in the local paper like a criminal.

My favorite story about Leah is the night I took her to my son's band concert. It was a cold, windy, rainy night, but she insisted that she attend. On my way to get her, I turned the seat warmer on low to warm her seat. After the concert, Ryan started my car and turned the seat warmer on but he left it on high. About one mile down the road Leah started squirming in her seat yelling, "Something's getting hot down here!"

I tried to explain how to turn off the seat warmer, but she couldn't find the button. She squirmed and wiggled in her seat the entire drive home. She survived her bun toasting incident and it makes me laugh every time I recall the episode.

In spite of her mishaps and funny stories, Leah was a dedicated lady. Her dedication to her family, friends, and God was evident in her life. When she passed away many years ago, we heard numerous stories of how she visited friends. She faithfully delivered her canned peaches, homemade applesauce, pies, frozen corn, corn on the cob, pickled beets, and such. She was on the go but none of us realized where she was going or what she was doing. She was thoughtful and caring to others as she lived out her life's mission to the fullest. Leah was not only dedicated to her grandchildren; she was dedicated to others. She spread God's love with her homemade treats and fresh produce which she shared with many friends.

Leah lived a life worthy of *Proverbs 3:3, "Never let loyalty and kindness leave you! Tie them around your neck as a reminder. Write them deep within your heart."* Her dedication to serve others and sow seeds of kindness was her life's goal. It didn't matter if it was friends or family, she was there. She cooked, canned, and baked to spread a little kindness to everyone. She wrote letters and sent care packages to college students. She even survived toasted buns and a speeding ticket to let her grandchildren know how much she loved them.

"Loyalty makes a person attractive." (Proverbs 19:22). Leah was attractive to her friends and family because of her loyalty and her love. Friends were delighted when she came to visit. Leah delivered her gifts with a smile, listened to their woes, and offered a heart full of kindness like no other.

Not everyone has the dedication to care for friends and family like Leah. I challenge you to find your niche in life, dedicate your talent to the Lord, and live your life to the fullest as you spread the love of Jesus to others.

Excerpt from *Live Life in Full Bloom*

Read more of my favorite devotions from *Live Life in Full Bloom* at www.maryrodman.com/BookBonus. These free devotions from the *Bloom Daily Devotional Series* will teach you to align your dreams with God's will for your life.

Mary Rodman

Lesson 3: A Free Woman

Christ set Mary Magdalene free from seven demons! As a result of this freedom, she continually shows her appreciation for God's sovereignty. This dramatic change in her life continually brought her back to the feet of her Savior. Her newly found freedom, combined with her servant's heart and financial abilities made her a thankful, behind the scenes worker for Jesus!

Many of us take the freedom from our sins for granted. God's grace offers us this freedom so we no longer have to carry the burden of our sinful life. After Christ set Mary Magdalene free from seven demons, she never looked back. She continually looked forward as a servant of Christ.

Many feel as if the word freedom and the Ten Commandments cannot be used in the same sentence.

Read *Psalm 119:44-46*

1. How can the ten commandments, which God commands you to follow, give you freedom?

One of the definitions of freedom is: "personal liberty, as opposed to bondage or slavery[i]."

The law sets you free from bondage. Sin entered into the world with Adam and Eve, but with that sin comes guilt. The law gave the Israelites a set of rules to follow. Rules which proved there was only one true God, the One and only God, who rescued them from Egypt. So, the law gives you and I freedom to know right from wrong, setting us free from bondage. But Christ came to set us free from the law.

Read *Galatians 5:1*

This freedom doesn't give you free will to do as you desire. If that were the case, you would be right back where you started, oppressed with guilt because of your sins. The freedom Christ offers is forgiveness of your sins. He offers you freedom to love and to serve others and when you mess up there is grace.

Mary Magdalene is a biblical example of this freedom. She was a servant of Christ because of her freedom. She no longer worried about the laws and the regulations set down by the High Counsel. She was free to follow and serve her Savior. She was free to love like Jesus loves. She was free to support Him financially. She was free to be part of His road crew. She was free from all of her sins. She knew the true meaning of GRACE! Her life is an example which teaches you how to serve with a grateful heart.

2. Has freedom given you the ability to serve others? Explain your answer.

Read *Romans 6:14*

The beauty of this freedom is God's grace. He knows you can't get it right and that you will always struggle with sin. His plan of salvation covers your sin with the blood of Christ.

Read *Romans 7:18-25*

Even Paul struggled to do what was right on a daily basis, but he kept his eyes on the prize, which is the grace of Jesus Christ. Sin comes in many different forms and each of us struggles in our own way.

3. In your journal, list a few of the sinful areas in which you struggle. (You may or may not want to share these with a group at this time, and that is okay.)

Read *Galatians 3:22*

4. Where does this scripture say you can find freedom from your sins?

Read *1 Timothy 2:5-6a*

5. Have you found freedom in the Savior? Explain.

Jesus Christ offers us this wonderful gift of grace. No one else can ever do this, because there is only one God and one Savior.

Mary Magdalene put her faith in Christ when He healed her from seven demons. Christ offers this free gift of salvation to all who call on His name.

As a young teenager, I accepted this gift of grace. Over the years, I have struggled and stumbled many times. None of us are perfect. We **all** struggle with sin in our lives.

Even those who feel as if they are sinless have sin, because that in itself is a sin.

Read *1 John 1:8-10*

Read *Galatians 5:13*

Grace sets us free and that grace makes all the difference in our lives! Freedom given by our Savior—gives us the ability to serve others in love! What a glorious discovery!

Mary Magdalene understood these truths and applied them to her life. She was an example of freedom because she served others with a thankful heart.

Your Challenge

Memorize the life changing verse below. It will serve as a reminder that the freedom from your sins, leads to a desire to know and follow Christ Jesus more. (Please write and memorize the version of the Bible you prefer.)

And now, just as you accepted Christ Jesus as your Lord, you must continue to follow him. Let your roots grow down into him, and let your lives be built on him. Then your faith will grow strong in the truth you were taught, and you will overflow with thankfulness. Colossians 2:6-7

Journal your thoughts on this lesson.

Shattered Window

We have a horizontal decorative window which is about eight feet long and one foot high above three vertical windows in our office. As I walked into the office one day, I noticed the window was shattered. I initially thought a bird hit the window, but the inside pane is the one broken. Therefore, the reason for the broken window remains a mystery.

The shattered pattern on the window looks like butterfly wings, without a body. It started almost exactly in the center of the window, and grew up and out into a beautiful pattern. Each time I enter the office, I look at the window. It is such a wonderful example of our shattered lives. Like the window, we are broken. Sometimes we feel as if our lives are shattered into hundreds or thousands of little pieces. Shattered marriages. Shattered families. Shattered health. Shattered churches. Shattered finances. So many broken pieces that we don't know how to put our lives back together again. But no matter how shattered we feel, God will turn our broken lives into beauty. He puts the pieces back together in a masterpiece which only He can create.

The pattern of the butterfly wings in the window reminds me of a new creation. *"This means that anyone who belongs to Christ has become a new person. The old life is gone; a new life has begun!" (2 Corinthians 5:17)*. Christ takes all the pieces of your shattered life and makes you a new person. First comes the forgiveness of your sins. He changes you on the inside. You think and act differently because you are now guided by the Holy Spirit. Many people

23

today say you are reformed or rehabilitated, but Christ says you are recreated. Like a butterfly who emerges from a cocoon, He takes those shattered pieces of your life and makes you into a beautiful person.

You no longer live a self-centered life. You now live for Christ as a new creation. *(2 Corinthians 5:15)*. A life where you begin to think and act more Christ-like. A life where God takes all of your shattered pieces and creates you into a beautiful person who lives for Christ.

As you walk this new journey with Christ, *"Let your roots grow down into him, and let your lives be built on him. Then your faith will grow strong in the truth you were taught, and you will overflow with thankfulness." (Colossians 2:7)*.

Like our broken window, the reason for your brokenness may always be a mystery. You may never know why God allowed you to walk through such pain and suffering. But you can cling to His promises. God will turn your shattered life into a masterpiece. One which only a Sovereign God can create.

Excerpt from *Live Life in Full Bloom*

As a speaker, Mary is known for her humor, and inspirational messages which challenge you to walk daily with Jesus. Book Mary for your next event at www.MaryRodman.com.

Lesson 4: A Thankful Woman

Christ made a miraculous change in the life of Mary Magdalene. From the moment she was healed of her demons, everything Mary accomplished and everything she felt, was with a thankful heart. Her gratitude is what allowed her to do what most of the disciples could not.

Out of fear, all of the disciples except John fled the scene during the crucifixion. Only John, Mary the mother of Jesus, and Mary Magdalene remained at the foot of the cross.

Mary Magdalene's heart was so grateful, she couldn't leave her Savior. She didn't fear for her life and scatter with the others. She stayed at the foot of the cross with a broken heart as Jesus suffered on crucifixion day.

How hard it must have been for her to witness the agony Jesus felt on the cross. But her selfless, thankful, servant's heart kept her right there, at the foot of the cross, until the bitter end!

Mary's heart overflowed with gratitude for her Savior. She never abandoned Him for even a second. She was there when Christ was nailed to the cross, and she was there when He cried out His final words, *"It is finished!"* This wonderful disciple of Christ was there, when *"He bowed His head and released His spirit." (John 19:30)*.

1. Think of a time in your life when you felt deep gratitude toward another person. Did you express your gratitude easily or is expressing gratitude difficult for you and why?

Let's take a step back into the Old Testament and look at the story of Ruth and Naomi. Ruth is a person of great character. She willingly walks away from her homeland of Moab, and travels with Naomi to Judah. Naomi tries to persuade Ruth to stay, but she refuses. With a grateful heart, she stays with her mother-in-law.

Read *Ruth 1:16-18*

Ruth not only walked away from the life she knew, she walked into difficult times. She and Naomi were both widows with no means of providing for themselves. In order to find food, Ruth gathered grain behind the harvesters.

> *"Wherever you go, I will go; wherever you live, I will live. Your people will be my people, and your God will be my God." (Ruth 1:16).*

2. If you were Ruth who had to work so hard for your food, would you still be clinging to the words you spoke earlier? Explain.

Read *Ruth 2:8-12*

As a foreigner in the land, Ruth's reputation preceded her. She was known as the foreigner who was hardworking, loving, kind, and faithful to her mother-in-law. She was a woman of great character. In spite of the hardships she and Naomi faced, she expresses her gratitude to Boaz who allowed her to glean in his fields. In return Boaz blesses her life.

3. What similarities do you see between Ruth and Mary Magdalene?

Both Ruth and Mary Magdalene served with a thankful heart. They were known for putting the needs of others first. Ruth, because she worked in the fields to provide food for Naomi and herself. Mary, as part of Jesus' road crew working behind the scenes and by sitting at the foot of the cross when Jesus was crucified.

Both of these ladies found their strength through God. Ruth openly declares, *"Your God will be my God." (Ruth 1:16).* She became an example of faith, hope and love as she gleaned the fields for food out of love for her mother-in-law.

Mary Magdalene was free to serve others with a grateful heart. That same grateful heart led her to the foot of the cross on crucifixion day, where she once again claimed Christ as her Savior. Nothing could keep these ladies from witnessing to the greatness of God.

Read *1 Timothy 1:12*

4. God calls each of us to be a servant. Why is there a difference between serving and serving with a thankful heart?

Yes, God calls you to serve, but with a grateful heart. It isn't about how many meals you take to shut-ins, or how many church committees on which you serve. God looks at the heart, so follow the example of Ruth and Mary Magdalene, and serve with a thankful heart.

Your Challenge

Journal some of your blessings in life. Write a prayer of gratitude to Christ for all He has given you.

Journal your thoughts on this lesson.

Well Done

We have the best dog in the world. We really do. Now on occasion she decides to remove boxes and other items from the garage and makes a mess in the yard. But as far as being a faithful dog, she is the best! When we moved a few miles down the road, we were concerned Bailey would travel back up the road to the farm and not stay home. She knew her boundaries on the farm and never left home. Upon her arrival, I walked her around the perimeter of our property and told her she was a good dog. The first night, we shut her in the shop so we wouldn't worry. The second night we let her sleep outside as usual. As we expected, she was right outside the door in the morning. A simple walk around her boundary line, and a little daytime exploring made her feel right at home. To our knowledge, she hasn't left the property since, except for the occasional dreaded trip to the vet.

This morning she walked with me to the barn to put out food for her and the cats, which is our typical routine. I then decided to go for a walk, so I rounded the house and headed down the driveway. Without me saying a word, Bailey stopped at the tree which is her boundary line. Upon my return, there she was faithfully waiting. I called out to her, "Well done, you are such a good dog."

She wagged her tail, grabbed her pop bottle to play, and off we went to the deck. To her it was worth the wait just to have a little play time.

His master replied, 'Well done, good and faithful servant! You have been faithful with a few things; I will put you in charge of many things. Come and share your master's happiness!' (Matthew 25:21 NIV).

Well done, my good and faithful servant. Can Jesus say this about your life? Bailey knows her boundaries, but do we? We like to test God, push rules to the limit, and twist the truth slightly to fit our needs. God has blessed us with intelligence and the ability to reason. Along with that He also gave us free will to make choices. Fortunately, when we make bad decisions, He gives us grace to cover our mistakes. None of us are perfect, but we need to strive to do better on a daily basis. Better at serving Christ, and better at helping others.

God rewards us with praise, just as I do Bailey. I told her she did a good job, and gave her a pat on the head. As a reward, we played fetch for a few minutes. These are all things she loves.

God loves to bless His children in the same manner. When we reach out to someone in need, we are blessed with a filled heart from serving others. When we pray for others, we are blessed by spending time with God. Each day is different, and each day God puts opportunities in front of us to witness. In order to recognize these moments, we simply need to slow down our lives, and live in the boundaries God sets. In other words, sit by our tree waiting, and listen for the Master. We need to practice the words of *Psalm 37:7a, "Be still in the presence of the LORD, and wait patiently for him to act."*

Take a few moments before starting your day and ask God for the opportunity to minister to someone today. When your day comes to an end, take time to pray. Thank God for the blessing of serving Him and ask forgiveness for any opportunities you may have missed along the way. As you listen to God, I am sure you will hear Him say, "Well done, my good and faithful servant! Wait until you see what I have planned for you tomorrow!"

Excerpt from *Bloom Where You're Planted*

When publishing the second edition of *Bloom Where You're Planted*, I discovered a miscount in the number of devotions. Instead of 99, there were actually 100 devotions. I omitted the first devotion ever written from the second edition to maintain my theme of 99. I didn't select this devotion because it wasn't as good as others, but because it is dear to my heart. You can receive the free devotion *Fall Harvest* at www.MaryRodman.com/BookBonus.

Lesson 5: A Witness for Christ

Mary Magdalene's faithfulness didn't end at the foot of the cross. Yes, she was grief stricken, but she was also mission driven. As soon as the Sabbath was over, she rushed to the tomb at daybreak to anoint Jesus' body with the proper burial spices.

She and the other ladies were worried about who would roll the large stone away from the tomb, but when they arrived, they found an open tomb.

Read *John 20:11-17*

The instant Jesus said, "Mary," she knew her Teacher, her Friend, her Savior was alive. He had risen from the dead.

1. Recall a moment in your life when you felt the presence of Christ. How did you know without a doubt He was with you?

Jesus blessed Mary on resurrection morning by choosing her to be the first witness of His resurrection. Christ knew of her financial support to His ministry. He was aware of her hard work behind the scenes. He saw her at the foot of the cross the day He was crucified, and He knew she would come to the grave following Passover. Yes, Christ saw her many activities, but more importantly Christ saw her heart.

When He looked at Mary Magdalene, He didn't see the person who was once filled with demons. What Jesus saw was the person she had become. A grateful follower, and a wonderful woman who was free to love and serve others.

2. How would you have reacted at the tomb that morning? Would you have willingly been the first person to admit that Jesus was alive?

3. How did each of these people react when God called them to be His servant?

Jonah - Read *Jonah 1:1-3*

Gideon - Read *Judges 6:36-40*

Mary - Read *Luke 24:8-12*

4. When you feel the nudge of the Holy Spirit to be a witness, who are you most like? Jonah, Gideon, or Mary Magdalene. Explain your answer?

Ultimately Gideon and Jonah trusted God and accomplished the tasks at hand. We each react differently under these circumstances, but in order for us to become more resilient, we need to follow the example of Mary

Magdalene. We need to tap into our deep faith and follow Jesus without question.

Mary's faith continued to grow even at the tomb. She didn't hesitate when Jesus sent her to tell the disciples that He was alive. She did exactly as He requested, and ran to tell the disciples the wonderful news, *"Christ is risen!"* How did she believe so easily and not question His resurrection?

Read *Luke 24:5-8*

She believed because she spent time learning from Jesus. She remembered Him saying that He would rise again on the third day. Like Mary Magdalene, do you believe? Are you all in for Jesus, or do you hesitate or try to run the other way? Witnessing can be difficult, but when you walk by faith and trust in the Word of God, you become a resilient woman of Christ.

5. Do you turn to God for strength or do you rely on friends and family? Why?

Read *Isaiah 40:27-31*

God never grows weary. Therefore, He is your only source of strength on difficult days. When you have a Father-Daughter relationship with Him, He will give you strength to be His witness to a lost world.

Your true source of strength in all circumstances does not come from family or friends. It can only come from Christ. Claim the following verse as truth in your life. Memorize it. Repeat it daily. Post it around your house if you desire. When you grasp this concept—when you understand that God is always with you—it will change your life forever.

> *"Never will I leave you; never will I forsake you."*
> *(Hebrews 13:5b (NIV)).*[ii]

The day Mary Magdalene was healed of her demons, she found that power and believed that Christ was always with her. She walked with Christ because she was *A Woman of Resilience.*

- She gave of her wealth, not because she had to, but out of gratefulness to her Savior. (Lesson 1).
- She served Christ and others with love, because He first loved her. (Lesson 2).
- She acknowledged Christ as her Savior and claimed her new life of freedom. (Lesson 3).
- She lived a life of love and gratitude because Jesus was her source of strength. (Lesson 4).
- She was a witness to her risen Savior because she was all in for Christ. (Lesson 5).

The definition of resilient is: Recovering readily from illness, depression, adversity or the like; buoyant.[iii]

Read *John 14:1, 15-17*

Resilience comes when you understand that God the Father, God the Son, and God the Holy Spirit are always with you. Mary Magdalene didn't become a resilient woman overnight. She became resilient because she walked with Jesus **daily**.

During difficult days, trials in life, illness, and just your day-to-day routine, tap into the strength which can only be found in Christ. His power is freely available and endless. When you truly understand that Jesus is always by your side, you become a witness of His greatness to the world. When you love with a grateful servant's heart, you will become—*A Woman of Resilience*.

Love like Mary Magdalene loved, because **Resilient Women**…

Give financially. They don't give out of obligation, they give out of love.

Serve others. Christ humbled himself and came to serve others out of love. Likewise, we need to follow His example and serve with love.

Embrace freedom. Freedom is found in the grace of Jesus Christ. Latch on to your freedom and love others as Christ loves you.

Show Gratitude. A heart full of appreciation is a heart full of love.

Witness for Jesus. Share your story. Share your source of hope which is found in Christ, and share your love with others.

Take the necessary steps each day to find strength in Jesus, because Jesus is love and resilient woman have an irrepressible passion for Jesus and others.

"And now these three remain: faith, hope and love. But the greatest of these is love."
1 Corinthians 13:13

Your Challenge

What changes do you need to make in your life to become *A Woman of Resilience*?

Journal your thoughts on this lesson.

Eyes of a Child

It is often said, "Beauty is in the eye of the beholder," and today was no exception. My granddaughters were picking a bouquet for their mom from the few remaining snapdragon blossoms. I felt as if their bouquet was more stems than flowers, but to them the flowers were beautiful. I mentioned that it was time to cut the marigolds off, but they highly disagreed. I saw a dull brown dying patch of marigolds. They saw beautiful orange and yellow blossoms shining though the darkness.

There are times when we should look at the world through the eyes of a child. They see beauty around themselves and the good in life. As adults, many of us look at the darker side. As we grow older, the simplest of tasks become more difficult and maybe that begins to taint our outlook on life. The struggles we face as adults tend to weigh us down as well. Rather than seeing the beauty in each day, we focus on the work involved, or the negativity surrounding us.

Many women put a great deal of emphasis on their physical beauty. So, the aging process often leaves us feeling less attractive than in our younger days. Peter tells us that our outward beauty should not be a priority in life. Our true beauty comes from within our souls. Since that beauty is from the Holy Spirit, we should never allow it to fade over time. We need to be diligent about caring for our souls in order for our inner beauty to shine.

Don't be concerned about the outward beauty of fancy hairstyles, expensive jewelry, or beautiful clothes. You should clothe yourselves instead with the beauty that comes from within, the unfading beauty of a gentle and quiet spirit, which is so precious to God. (1 Peter 3:3-4)

Is this not the same beauty I mentioned in the previous devotion, *He's My Dad?* *"The unfading beauty of a gentle and quiet spirit,"* is found by heeding the advice given in the Fruits of the Spirit. As a body of believers, our best witness is our attitude in life. If we are quick to argue, or have a bleak outlook on life, we are a poor witness for Christ.

Our lives should reflect the joy of the Lord through our gentle and quiet spirit. The more Christ-like we are, the better witnesses we become. It is often said, "Our actions speak louder than our words." To be a great disciple of Christ, we need to allow the Holy Spirit to fill our hearts with *"love, joy, peace, patience, kindness, goodness, faithfulness, gentleness, and self-control." (Galatians 5:22)*.

This devotional book is about the promises of God, and one of His greatest promises is that He will always be with us. *(Matthew 28:20)*. God is with you, so look at life through the eyes of a child and see the beauty which surrounds you. Allow yourself to look past the stems to find the snapdragon blossoms and past the dull brown dying marigolds for a glimpse of yellow and orange beauty each day.

Excerpt from devotional ***Bloom in God's Promises***

Bloom in God's Promises Sneak Peek contains devotions about counting your blessings. Rather than having a negative attitude in life, live a life full of gratitude like Mary Magdalene. Download this series at www.MaryRodman.com/SneakPeek

Mary Rodman

Resources

Bloom Daily Devotional Series Book 3, *Bloom in God's Promises* will be available in the future. Tidbits of encouragement from the book will be available on social media, or through www.MaryRodman.com/BookBonus.

Discount Purchases

- My gift to you—Enter coupon code **ThankYou** at www.MaryRodman.com/shop to receive a **one-time only 20% discount** on any purchases from my website. All devotionals will be signed before shipment.
- *Bloom Daily Devotional Series Book 1, Bloom Where You're Planted*
  "This beautifully written book is a delight, filled with wonderful stories from her life and awesome applications of God's truth. It will lift you up and speak words of truth and encouragement into your life." *~Doris Swift*
- *Bloom Daily Devotional Series Book 2, Live Life in Full Bloom*
  "A must-read devotional. Mary's words are from her heart. I can see every story, as if I was standing there watching it happen. I laughed so hard at some of the stories because, life happens. ~TGJ – Amazon Customer

- *Bloom Daily Devotional Series Book 3, Bloom in God's Promises*
  General reading and women's Bible study. Just a wonderful writing style. Uplifting. It makes you giggle from your own relatable experiences. ~Amazon July 2021, dkj
- *Bloom Daily Devotional Series Journals* Include a quote from each devotion and a place to journal your thoughts, including a Daily Gratitude section. The journals are only available at https://MaryRodman.com/shop

Download free Resources for your next event
- Free devotions from *Bloom in God's Promises* at www.MaryRodman.com/SneakPeek

  Bloom in God's Promises Sneak Peek We often develop a negative attitude rather than counting our blessings. These devotions will help you look at the good side of life.
- Download free devotions from *Live Life in Full Bloom* at www.MaryRodman.com/BookBonus

  Live Life in Full Bloom Favorites. Devotions to help you see gratitude in your life and focus on God's will each day.
- Download free devotionals from *Bloom Where You're Planted* at www.MaryRodman.com/BookBonuses.

  "Blessings" God blesses our lives every day. We need to continually watch for those blessings in the midst of our chaos.

Book Mary as a Speaker-Facilitator for your weekend retreat at www.MaryRodman.com/speaking

- **Who Are You? Discover the Woman God Created You to Be** *"There are many virtuous and capable women in the world, but you surpass them all!" (Proverbs 31:29)*
- Mary's retreat will transform your walk with Christ as she shares her funny stories, biblical examples, and powerful messages through these four topics.

   Defining Moments Within minutes, the Woman caught in adultery had both good and bad defining moments in her life. The moment she was dragged into public and humiliated, and the moment Jesus said, "Go and sin no more." Mary will challenge you to see both bad and good defining moments as good, when used for God's glory.

   God Loves You The Samaritan Woman made many mistakes in her life, yet Jesus pursued her until she understood she was loved by the Savior of the world. Mary's words of encouragement will challenge you to serve Christ regardless of your past mistakes.

   Who Are You? Mary Magdalene was possessed by seven evil spirits. Christ changed her life dramatically and she understood who she was in Christ and how to serve her Savior.

   Dare to Dream Caleb dreamed of the Promised Land for over forty years, but patiently waited for the Lord to lead the battle to conquer the land. Your dreams will also come into fruition, when you align your dreams with God's will for your life.

- This weekend retreat is available in multiple formats.
  - o Mary as a speaker. She will present the four talks and provide breakout questions for your small group leaders in advance.
  - o Mary as both the speaker and the facilitator for your event.
  - o Optional music by Angie Howard. Angie's musical talent as a worship leader and soloist is uplifting and inspirational.

Book Mary as a keynote speaker for your next event. Her topics include...

- **Something Out of Nothing** The loss of four family members in five years sent Mary into a season of grief. Grief is a true pain which sometimes feels unbearable. She shares how she made something out of nothing to move on with her life.
- ***Dare to Dream*** *Your dreams are simply dreams, unless we align them with God's will for your life. Mary will challenge you to accomplish great ministry when the Lord is with you. "What you dare to dream of, dare to do." Sarah Jane Shoaf.*
- ***Bloom Where You're Planted*** *From a wild ride down the mountainside to the heartaches of life, Mary shares how to BLOOM in all aspects of your life.*

- ***The Woman God Sees*** *God sees you as His chosen, precious, beloved, royalty. Learn how "the Lord delights in you. (Isaiah 62:4)." through Mary's personal stories intertwined with scripture.*

- ***A Christian Farm Wife's Perspective*** *As a newlywed on the farm Mary soon realized her life was much different than it was growing up on a dairy farm. She shares some of her stressful moments and how a Christ centered marriage makes a difference as they worked together.*

- ***Faith, Farming or Career?*** *Do you ever wonder which direction to turn? Why not include them all? Mary's strong faith is the pivotal point which merges her farm life with her career as a Christian writer and speaker. She shares farm statistics to increase awareness of the family farm along with her stories of strong faith as encouragement.*

- ***Custom Topic*** *Mary enjoys Bible research and sharing some of the antics from her life. She is open to speaking opportunities on your topic of choice. Please allow six-weeks preparation time, unless prior arrangements have been made. For more information go to www.MaryRodman.com/speaking.*

More Books and Resources
by Mary Rodman

Stay in touch by using our messenger's treasury of transformational inspiration, insight, and guidance. **Download and join** the free *Inspire U app* for additional personal resources on your mobile device today!

Enjoy videos I recorded and placed in The Inspire U app associated with this book. They will bring you more insight into the 5 lessons and Irrepressible Grace.

Did you enjoy *Mary Magdalene a Woman of Resilience?*
Then you should read
Cast the First Stone be Transformed by Grace

There she was in the public square being mocked and disgraced. Shame surrounded her like a cloud which would never lift. Did she know enough about God to question His sovereignty? You talk about your bad defining moments in life—this one tops them all!

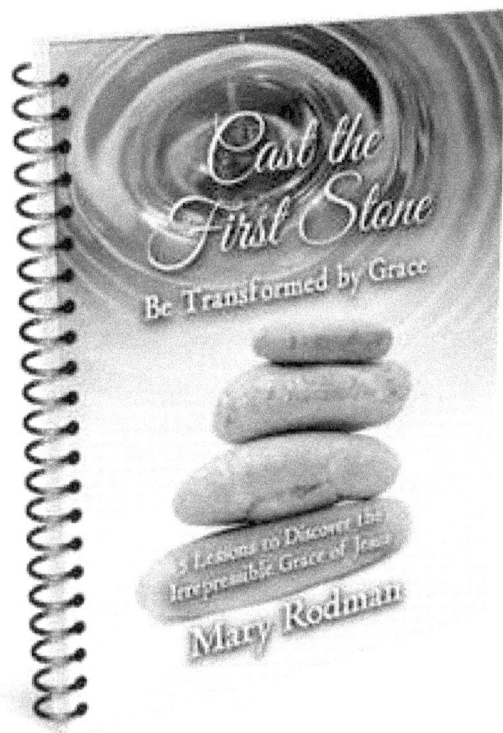

Bloom Daily Devotional Series Journals are only available at https://MaryRodman.com/shop.

All other books are available on her website or a distributor of your choice in paperback and eBook

Bloom Where You're Planted

Through laughter, memories and even sorrow, Mary helps you see the Bright Morning Star, named Jesus. Discover her humor in the devotional Bird Poop, as she highlights the Biblical example of Abigail and how you might handle unwelcome life circumstances.

***Bloom Where You're Planted* is available in 2 different editions with the same great messages.**

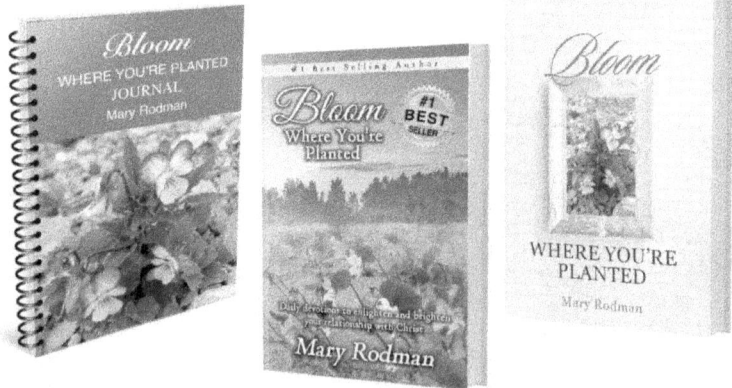

Live Life in Full Bloom.

Chuckle as Mary shares her rotisserie experience at the sleep clinic, ad how she was humbly reminded of the blessings in her life which she had taken for granted.

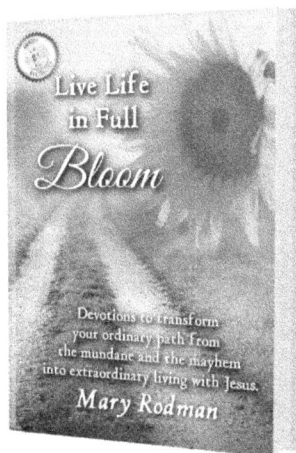

Bloom In God's Promises!

Read Mary's award winning devotional, "Happy Place." Picture in your mind your happy place…where you are calm, your troubles are few, and you have a peaceful smile on your face. You see someone walking toward you, but you don't recognize Him. This man calls out to you, and suddenly you realize…

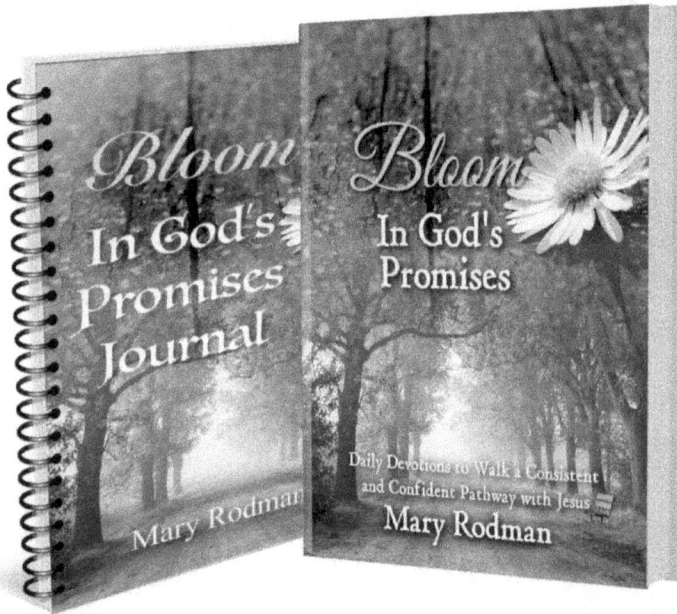

About the Author

Mary resides in Radnor, Ohio with her husband, Jim. Together they enjoy farm life, hard work, vacations, family and friends. She is a farm girl who discovered her niche as a Christian author and speaker. Mary loves sharing about the Lord through both her written and spoken words. Mary's life is an open book as she shares her joys, struggles and embarrassing moments.

As a Christian author and speaker, Mary's objective is to point you toward Jesus. Her words are simple, and her examples are relatable, but when Jesus touches your heart it is amazing. When you follow Him wholeheartedly, and align your dreams with God's will, the outcome is life altering.

The first goal of Mary's ministry is to offer you encouragement and inspiration. She is a "seed planter." The person who sees a glimmer of hope in the small day-to-day routines of life. Therefore, the key verse for her ministry is: *"When we get together, I want to encourage you in your faith, but I also want to be encouraged by yours." (Romans 1:12).*

Once the seed of hope is planted in your heart, Mary motivates you to stay in God's Word to seek wisdom, and learn more about Jesus' amazing grace. *"If you need wisdom, ask our generous God, and he will give it to you. He will not rebuke you for asking." (James 1:5).*

Mary's prayer is that you have a personal relationship with our Redeemer, because when you Bloom with Jesus, you become a child of God who is cultivated for your beauty. This beauty does not happen overnight, it is a gradual change within your soul, because of your relationship with Jesus.

For more information of God's grace, go to https://maryrodman.com/gods-promises/[1].

---

[1] https://maryrodman.com/gods-promises/

About The Publisher

We love helping heart-centered, Christian-principled aspiring writers, and new authors tell your compelling stories and showcase your excellence like no other. Our publishing ministry is designed to help you whether you've already written your book, or it's still a vision or a dream.

Our Promise

You retain full control over your manuscripts, cover design, and editing options. You may publish your completed project in any or all formats available. You retain full copyright privileges to all manuscripts, cover designs, or other print materials produced while working with us. You retain the freedom to publish in all languages, globally.

Legacy Lane Publishing
www.LegacyLanePublisng.com[2]

---

[2] https://LegacyLanePublishing.com

---

[i] "Dictionary.com." Dictionary.com. Accessed March 06, 2019. https://www.dictionary.com/.

[ii] Holy Bible, New International Version®, NIV® Copyright ©1973, 1978, 1984, 2011 by Biblica, Inc.® Used by permission. All rights reserved worldwide.

[iiiii] "Dictionary.com." Dictionary.com. Accessed March 06, 2019. https://www.dictionary.com/.